MW01195869

LEAD THE CATEGORY!

LEAD THE CATEGORY!

Stan Berenbaum

The Secrets of Franchising and Business Success

iUniverse, Inc.
New York Bloomington

Lead the Category!
The Secrets of Franchising and Business Success

Copyright © 2009 by Stan Berenbaum

All rights reserved. No part of this book may be used or reproduced by any means, graphic, electronic, or mechanical, including photocopying, recording, taping or by any information storage retrieval system without the written permission of the publisher except in the case of brief quotations embodied in critical articles and reviews.

iUniverse books may be ordered through booksellers or by contacting:

iUniverse
1663 Liberty Drive
Bloomington, IN 47403
www.iuniverse.com
1-800-Authors (1-800-288-4677)

Because of the dynamic nature of the Internet, any Web addresses or links contained in this book may have changed since publication and may no longer be valid. The views expressed in this work are solely those of the author and do not necessarily reflect the views of the publisher, and the publisher hereby disclaims any responsibility for them.

ISBN: 978-1-4401-3228-5 (pbk)
ISBN: 978-1-4401-3230-8 (dj)
ISBN: 978-1-4401-3229-2 (ebk)

Printed in the United States of America
iUniverse rev. date: 4/24/09

Dedication

To my wife Kathryn, who would like me to try some of these ideas at home.

"The only thing that shatters dreams is compromise."

Richard Bach

Contents

Introduction

As an attorney and executive, I've had the opportunity to work with many category leaders, including Michael and Marian Ilitch of Little Caesar Enterprises, Inc. Little Caesars was just one of several companies in their family's multi-billion dollar sports, restaurant and entertainment portfolio.

Whenever Mr. Ilitch spoke, he had something important to say. Concepts such as quick wealth and flipping companies for short-term gain were not in his vocabulary. While he had amassed great wealth through hard work, he always remained modest, humble and successful, never having lost touch with the soccer mom, the blue-collar dad and the kids and families who visited his restaurants.

I offer this glance because in so many ways Mr. Ilitch and his family represent the positive power of franchising -- the successful building of a brand and system, sustainable job and wealth creation for their employees, franchisees and families, and the ability to give back to their communities through a variety of charitable endeavors.

I have since moved on from Little Caesars and am now president and CEO of another category leader, American Leak Detection, Inc., an international franchisor specializing in the non-invasive detection of water and other leaks.

So, what are the secrets of franchising and business success? And how do you become a category leader? Through this book,

I share some winning strategies, practical thoughts and easy to implement techniques so that you can become the leader in your category.

If any of the thoughts in this book have motivated or spoken to you, please contact me and share your story at spb@ stanberenbaum.com.

Regards,

Stan Berenbaum

Category Leaders
Communicate More Effectively

"The art of communication is the language of leadership."

James Humes

1. Deliver on a Specific Promise

Category leaders do not have fuzzy mission statements about providing customers with a great or quality product, with great service at a great or reasonable price.

Rather, they focus *and* deliver on a specific promise to their customer. At American Leak Detection, our promise is to show up on time, in uniform, find the leak non-invasively, and then clean up before we leave.

Takeaway: Are you focusing and delivering on a specific promise to your customer?

2. Half a Loaf

You ask your head of company operations, "How are sales?" "Great," he or she says. You ask your head of HR, "How is Joe, the new employee, working out?" "Great," he or she says.

Yet, you've heard this before.

Remember, everyone gives you "half a loaf" – an incomplete story. Always.

This is especially the case if you are in a senior leadership or management position at your company. Not surprisingly, your direct reports are not exactly anxious to share every piece of bad news with you.

Takeaway: To be a category leader you need to get the full story. So get it. Better yet, get the numbers (all of them). P&Ls don't lie.

3.   Excel, Flip Charts and PowerPoints

As a young attorney, I once wrote a memo for a company president who was going to share it with the company's owner. The memo concerned the buy-back of a number of franchised units and its likely impact on the company.

The president took my memo and then re-wrote it into Excel. It was then I learned that Excel is a language. So is a flip chart, a graph and a PowerPoint presentation.

Takeaway: To be a category leader, communicate in the manner most helpful to your target audience, *not to you.*

4.　Surveys, A Few Suggestions

A few suggestions for franchisors taking written surveys of their franchisees:

(a)　Keep it short.

(b)　Focus more on forward-looking questions (i.e., should we do "x" or "y"). Too much focus on backward-looking questions asking about "problems," the "relationship", how "we" the franchisor are doing or asking for a "grade" or "rating" from your franchisees, may sometimes be unhelpful and/or bog down forward progress.

(c)　Once you receive the information, share it. Then use it.

Takeaway: Category leaders know that surveys are only helpful if the results are actually shared and used.

5.   My Market Is Different

"My market is different," says the franchisee who may be resistant to a new idea, offering or campaign.

"Let me guess, says the franchisor -- it's hard for you to find good help. And, when you do, your employees don't stay long -- hard to compete against those other companies that pay more and offer health insurance and other benefits. And I know things are a bit rough. The economy is bad. Homes aren't selling. Everyone is cutting back. Gas, insurance and other costs keep escalating. And I understand things are a bit slow this time of year because [school just started] [school just ended] [it's the Holidays] [it's the middle of the summer] [it's the middle of the winter]. Additionally, I know that a new competitor just entered your market and is undercutting your prices. You know, you're right, your market is different."

Takeaway: While markets may differ, category leaders know that core business challenges remain the same. Next time your franchisee tells you he is resistant to a new idea because his market is different, uncover his core business challenges, as well as his unspoken objections and fears. Once identified, now you know where to start the conversation.

6.   What to Do

When a franchisee breaches the franchise agreement, do two things:

(a) document it, and

(b) offer to help.

Takeaway: Category leaders help their franchisees. They also document problems in the event breaches are not cured and litigation ensues.

7.   Be Thankful For Negative Postings

Some quick rules about franchisee postings on a franchisor's internal intranet:

(a) Franchisor corporate staff should respond quickly to questions and requests for assistance -- even if it is to say that you will be looking into the matter and getting back by a certain date. In addition to the belief that "corporate" is unresponsive to a franchisee's needs, the absence of a timely response to postings concerning system-wide concerns may lead to rumors and speculation.

(b) If there is a negative posting – be thankful. As a general rule, only 10% of your system posts questions or comments, positive or negative. When a negative comment is posted, it is likely that other franchisees have the same thoughts or concerns. Use the posting as an opportunity to address the issue constructively.

(c) As with all postings, be civil and respectful. When responding to a particularly negative posting, explain the situation and what you are doing to address it. If the franchisor has made a mistake or could have done better, simply say so.

(d) If a serious or personal matter is raised, send a message letting the posting franchisee and system know that you take the issue seriously and offer to call or meet the specific franchisee to discuss. Your goal here is to let the franchisee and system know that you intend to address the problem quickly and to then take the matter *off-line*. On-line and open-forum discussions concerning especially sensitive and franchisee-specific issues should usually be avoided.

Takeaway: Category leaders are thankful for negative postings.

8.   Friendly Persuasion

Some people are persuaded by facts and others by emotion. Still others are persuaded by an appeal to authority (i.e., "He's the boss"); an appeal to tradition ("That's the way we've always done it"); an appeal to precedent ("That's our policy"; "Those are the rules"); or an appeal to the public good ("We need to evolve our offerings because it's in the best interest of our system and customers").

Takeaway: When seeking to persuade, category leaders first listen. Then, they use those appeals that are most likely to support their position and resonate with others.

9.   It's All About Connecting

Franchisees and customers want the same thing – to feel a connection – to know that you personally care more about them than you do about your product or your service. As John Maxwell says, "People don't care how much you know--until they know how much you care."

Takeaway: To be a category leader, you need to connect with your franchisees and customers.

10.   So Do Franchisees

We learned in physics that nature abhors a vacuum. Well, so do franchisees. If a communication vacuum exists between a franchisor and franchisee, that vacuum will be filled – usually with rumors, speculation, concerns, and fear.

Takeaway: Don't allow communication vacuums.

11.   Is Transparency Your Goal?

Transparency is defined as a condition in which "nothing" is hidden.

Today's conventional wisdom is that transparency is good and that franchisors should be transparent with their franchisees.

Of course, transparency has many benefits. It helps create trust, accountability, responsibility and improved communication. It may even help to prevent corruption or other fraudulent conduct.

Indeed, the law already imposes a certain amount of transparency on franchisors, i.e., required disclosures under the FTC Rule and state franchising laws; laws prohibiting the making of false and/or misleading statements or omissions; and rules regarding the use of franchisee marketing funds.

Legal requirements aside, franchisors are bound to become more transparent simply as a result of our digital age where information is more readily accessible.

But is transparency your franchise company's goal? Probably not. Most likely, your goal is to serve customers, make money, produce a return for your stakeholders and ensure sustainable long-term success for your system. While this needs to be done ethically, it need not necessarily be done with transparency.

So if the above are your goals, the real question is whether transparency helps you achieve them.

As to this, each franchisor needs to make its own assessment. There may be times, for example, when a choice has to be made between speed to market on the one hand, and complete transparency with inefficiencies and slower processes on the other.

Additionally, the road to transparency sometimes seems one-way – with franchisees actually seeking greater disclosures from the franchisor but unwilling to always share in kind.

Most importantly, however, franchisors and franchisees need to understand that the seal of transparency is without warranty – there is no guarantee that transparency results in better decisions or even in decisions which are correct.

Interestingly, in two critical areas (jury deliberations and state and federal elections) society has opted for processes which are opaque as opposed to transparent. Juries deliberate in private; your vote for president is cast confidentially. In these cases, society has determined that open decisions could actually distort otherwise sound decision making processes.

Takeaway: Transparency has many benefits, but it is not necessarily your company's goal.

12. Communicate More by Saying Less

Many times, CEOs and executives feel the need to fill the silence. Don't. Say nothing. Let your employees do the talking at internal and external meetings, phone calls and conferences. Otherwise, you may be unknowingly conditioning your employees to remain silent to let the boss talk.

Takeaway: Communicate more by saying less.

13. Not Every Sentence Needs an Exclamation Point

At company-wide meetings, I would ask each department leader to provide an update – usually five or ten minutes in length. After the update, I found myself in the habit of inserting an "exclamation point" by adding a sentence or two on the update – amplifying certain points or slightly modifying others. While I thought this was helpful, I later found out that our leaders felt that this amplification took away from their update, their message and, at times, served to slightly contradict or correct them in public.

Takeaway: Not every sentence needs an exclamation point.

14.   Speeches, Don't!

To make your speeches more effective, do less "speech-making." Instead, tell a memorable story to illustrate your point.

Takeaway: While most people will forget the words you say, they'll remember and connect with the stories you tell.

15.   Jail Break

Perhaps the franchisor is meeting with its franchisee association or its advisory council. All have good intentions. Yet, the meeting soon breaks down, with each "side" taking "sides," as if each were playing roles that had been scripted for them.

Why does this happen?

In 1971, a study was conducted at Stanford University called the "Stanford prison experiment." In it, volunteers were assigned roles as either "prisoners" or "guards", with the basement of the Stanford psychology building serving as the "prison."

Very quickly, the "guards" assumed the identity of "guards" and the "prisoners" assumed the identity of "prisoners." One-third of the guards actually began to engage in cruel behavior – not permitting the "prisoners" to go the bathroom, making the "prisoners" stand nude in their "cells," or taking away the "prisoner's" mattresses. Many of the prisoners began to suffer emotional trauma and some were even planning an "escape." The study was then cut short.

In trying to explain the behavior of these volunteers, all of whom were "normal" only hours before the experiment began, some suggested that the volunteers were simply conforming their behavior to their situation. Thus, it was the situation that caused the volunteers to act the way that they did as opposed anything inherent in their own personalities.

If a lesson can be drawn from the Stanford prison experiment it is that situations matter. Thus, if you find your franchise association or advisory council meetings unproductive because you believe everyone is simply playing out their "role," then change the situation -- meet in smaller groups, meet individually, clear items in advance, bring in outside experts – do anything to change the situation – such that it can make for a more productive exchange.

Takeaway: Because situations matter, category leaders control the situation.

16.   The Game of Telephone Just Got Faster

Be aware that the game of "telephone," where a message is passed from one person to another – is both faster and more exaggerated in our electronic and time-crunched age of 24/7 cable, cell phones, Blackberrys and instant messaging.

Additionally, no one is immune. On March 10, 2008, rumors started circulating that Bear Stearns was having "liquidity" issues. While Bear Stearns did have problems in connection with the sub-prime mortgage crisis, liquidity was not one of them. Indeed, Bear had $18 billion in cash reserves and over $300 billion in total assets. Yet, the rumor caused a "run" on the investment bank. Only 6 days later, Bear Stearns was gone -- sold to JPMorgan Chase for 10% of its market value.

Takeaway: No one is immune from today's exaggerated and quicker game of telephone.

Category Leaders
Have More Effective Employees

"If you want to build a ship, don't drum up people together to collect wood and don't assign them tasks and work, but rather teach them to long for the sea."

Antoine de Saint-Exupery

17.   There Are Only Three Rules

There are only 3 employment rules: hire the right employee; train the employee to do the job; hold the employee accountable.

Most companies miss at least two of the three.

Takeaway: Category leaders follow the three rules of employment.

18.   Nordstrom

Nordstrom doesn't train people to be friendly; Nordstrom hires friendly people.

Takeaway: Hire right.

19.   Every Issue Is This

After you hire an employee, every issue you have with that employee is a training issue.

Takeaway: Never stop training.

20. Training, Get Real

Franchisor corporate staff, including the leadership team, should periodically train in their franchisee's business environment – whether it is the hamburger restaurant, the pizza store or the drycleaner.

In addition to really learning the business, it will help corporate connect and have a better relationship with its franchisees.

Takeaway: Category leaders have their corporate staff train in the "real" environment of their franchisee's business.

21.   Reverse Delegation

Delegation is usually good.

Reverse delegation (where you are doing a subordinate's work) is not.

Takeaway: If you are consistently engaged in reverse delegation (doing *his* job instead of *yours*), then identify why it is occurring (subordinate is either in need of training or is failing to perform his tasks) and resolve it.

22.   Conflation

A re-occurring issue with franchisor corporate staff is conflating the franchisor's business with the franchisee's business. "Corporate" may be in the franchising business. Franchisees are in the specific product or service business they are in.

Takeaway: Category leaders help franchisees in <u>their</u> business, not the business at corporate.

23. Technology -- It Is and It Isn't

Technology is important. It can give your company a tremendous competitive edge. Yet, it's really not the pizza oven that makes your pizza concept successful. Rather, it's always the people you have and the customer service and experience you provide.

Takeaway: It's not just the technology.

24.   Forget Motivation

Don't worry about "motivating" your employees or franchisees. Just avoid "de-motivating" them. De-motivation can take many forms including micro-managing, failing to train, not communicating, or bringing your personal problems and resulting "drama" to the office and to your franchise system.

For your employees, one of the more common ways of de-motivating them is to allow your franchisees or others to play "Ring Around The Rosie" – calling up the chain until they get the "answer" they want.

Takeaway: Stop de-motivating.

25.   The Org Chart Paradox

For many businesses, their most important employee is the one answering the phone and directly helping the customer. Yet, that employee may make the least amount of money and may be provided the least of amount of training.

Takeaway: Modify the pyramid.

26.   The Answer: Nine Billion Hours

If the answer is 9 billion hours, then the question is how much time is spent playing computer solitaire each year. As a point of reference -- this is over one thousand times the amount of time it took to build the Empire State Building.

Some of these computer solitaire hours occur at the workplace. Indeed, the amount of wasted time at some companies is staggering. If time is being wasted at your company, then of course you need to evaluate your workforce. You also, however, need to evaluate how fun your workplace is. Fun, by the way, doesn't mean party hats, noisemakers and a conga line. Rather, fun is where your employees feel engaged, excited and energized about the contributions they are making to your company.

Takeaway: There is always a positive correlation between long-term productivity and workplace enjoyment.

27. Point-Persons, Stock Up

Every company has at least one -- a point-person – the person your franchisees call when they need something done, regardless of the subject matter.

Takeaway: Category leaders stock their company full of point-persons.

28.   Don't Be Afraid of Turnover

Conventional wisdom is that low turnover is good. Yet, low turnover may lead to a company which becomes lethargic, stagnant and less innovative. Low-turnover may also mask problems, problems which have ways of eventually catching up with you.

Takeaway: Category leaders are not afraid of turnover.

29. Scrap Your Customer Service Department

Customer service, customer solutions, customer loyalty, and customer experience are not programs, checklists, departments or job titles. They are your *company* and *everyone* is responsible.

Training is key. At American Leak Detection, we have trained everyone on our team, not just those on our front line, on how to live and provide service solutions to our customers.

Takeaway: Customer service is not a department.

30.   Sure-Fire Rapid Advancement Strategy

Rapid advancement strategy for employees: quit focusing on "your" department's budget. Instead, find ways to improve overall company revenue and earnings.

Takeaway: Advance the company to advance yourself.

Category Leaders
Have More Effective Leaders

"Leadership is action, not position."

Donald McGannon

31. Take Charge

Category leaders don't leave the franchise relationship to chance. They take charge and ownership of it.

Takeaway: To be a category leader, you need to take charge of the franchise relationship.

32. Pull the Trigger

I asked a giant in franchising his secret of success. His answer: "I was never afraid to pull the trigger."

Takeaway: Many times, executives give too much weight to their professional advisors who list problems, risks, and "logical" reasons why not to move forward or take action. Next time, listen to your advisors. Find ways to reduce risk. Then, pull the trigger.

33.   Don't Wait

To be successful, category leaders know that they should not and cannot wait for:

- more working capital
- a governmental bailout
- a better economy
- better employees
- better franchisees
- next generation technology
- [insert excuse here]

Takeaway: Category leaders don't wait.

34.   Ultimately . . .

Just because you can delegate projects, functions and tasks doesn't mean that you can abdicate responsibility.

Takeaway: If you're the boss, you're ultimately responsible.

35. Connect the Dots

Frequently, executives will meet with their department heads and discuss updates on specific tasks.

On a regular basis, forget these meetings.

Instead, meet individually with all or as many of your employees as you can. Don't discuss the status of specific tasks. Instead, let the employee share his thoughts, strategies and ideas for growing the company.

Takeaway: As a leader, your job is to connect and prioritize the idea-dots across your company and system.

36.   That's Why I Hired You

A group of franchisees were complaining about an issue that related to the Chairman. Because the complaints kept coming in, I decided to complain to the Chairman, asking the Chairman was he was going to do.

"Nothing," he said, "that's why I hired *you*."

Takeaway: Your job is to solve problems, not simply pass them up-line, down-line or sideways.

37. Change

As Tom Feltenstein says in his new book, *Change is Good, You Go First,* forget your past successes, simplify your message and focus on your customers. If you don't like change, then, Tom says, you'll like irrelevancy a lot less.

Takeaway: Category leaders know that they need to continue evolving or risk irrelevancy.

38.   It's Not That Difficult

Avoid people who over-complicate or are too clever. Remember, people want to do business with those who can explain what they do and the value they provide in a simple and straightforward way.

Red flags should go up when you hear too much about parallel processing and the meshing of someone's killer ROI, their extension of 24/365 functionalities, their benchmarking of best of breed/next-generation bleeding-edge paradigms, and their incubation of B2C web-readiness.

Takeaway: To be a category leader, don't be too clever.

39.   Taking Care of Your Numbers

As a leader, meeting your numbers doesn't guarantee you a passing grade. In today's post-Enron/sub-prime mortgage world, everyone wants a say in how you run your business, including shareholders, franchisees, employees, directors, state franchise regulators, the federal government, lenders and private equity. Leadership requires that you not only make your numbers, but that you steer the course while listening, seeking advice from, and answering to a variety of constituents.

Takeaway: Category leaders know that making your numbers is no longer enough.

40.   What You Think of Me

While the best franchise leaders listen and communicate with their franchisees, they are not overly concerned with what franchisees think of them. Being unconcerned with day-to-day "polls" allows these leaders the freedom to focus on and implement continuous and long-term system-wide improvement.

Takeaway: Don't' be unduly concerned with day-to-day polls.

41.   5 or 10 Minutes

I studied music in college and almost majored in it. At the time, I was taking lessons from the principal clarinetist of the Detroit Symphony Orchestra. One day, he asked me how often I practiced. I began to tell him (i.e., excuse, excuse) that I had difficulty finding large blocks of practice time.

I'll never forget his answer – "Stan," he said, "when you have five or ten minutes of free time -- just practice."

Takeaway: Too many people wait to do the "big" or "important" project (or write the article, read the book, or learn the new skill) until they clear the desk and get an afternoon of free time. It just doesn't happen. Instead, try living your life in 5 or 10 minute increments.

42.   Humility

To be successful you don't need to prove that you know the answer to every question. When you need help – be it from an expert on franchising, the super-franchise or business lawyer or the marketing specialist – get it.

Takeaway: Category leaders stay humble and get help when needed.

43.   Crowds

Good leaders stand out from the crowd. Great leaders sometimes seem to avoid the crowd. Said another way, "The man who follows a crowd will never be followed by a crowd." R.S. Donnell

Takeaway: Sometimes, it's better to avoid the crowds.

44. Second, Third and Fourth Guessing

You will be second-guessed. Often.

Helpful formula: good judgment = taking action after you collect information and review the facts.

No matter how fast or slow you make your decision, the key here is to avoid making (or being perceived to have made) a knee-jerk reaction.

Takeaway: Category leaders get and review the facts first.

45.   Tic, Tic, Tic

Some leaders are late for every appointment, phone call, meeting and flight.

Are they successful? Yes – in upsetting just about everyone who works and does business with them.

Negative consequences follow.

Takeaway: Credibility starts with timeliness.

46. Hope, Don't (always)

Hope is important. It keeps people alive and going during tough times.

Occasionally, though, think beyond hope. Instead, no matter your circumstance, try living, working and enjoying the present moment.

Takeaway: Category leaders use the present moment.

47.   Not Happy?

If you're not happy, but don't know where to start, ask yourself what are you tolerating?

Takeaway: Sometimes the only thing that shatters dreams is compromise.

48.   Your Seven Iron

February in Detroit can be cold, gray and dreary. One February, on a visit to Palm Springs, California, I took out my golf clubs. I was inspired by the clean air, 75 degree weather, blue skies and mountains. While inspired, my game was no different than in Detroit – less than respectable. It was then I learned that wherever you are, you take your golf game with you.

Takeaway: Certain people try to escape problems, be it a boss, bad relationship, a co-worker, a franchise system, or a failed career by going elsewhere. After going elsewhere, however, the same set of problems for these people soon re-emerge. Remember, wherever you are, you take yourself with you.

49.   A Grain of Sand

When progress slows, don't always ascribe the cause to a huge barrier or obstacle. As Robert Service says, "It isn't the mountain ahead that wears you out--it's the grain of sand in your shoe."

Takeaway: Category leaders find and eliminate the "grains of sand" blocking their progress.

50. Nothing, Unless You Get Caught

Conversation between a lawyer and his client concerning proposed conduct which may be or arguably is beyond the gray zone:

Client: What happens if our company does this?

Lawyer: Nothing, unless you get caught.

Client: What happens if we get caught?

Lawyer: Sh@t hits the fan.

Client: So you saying we shouldn't do this?

Lawyer: Right.

Takeaway: If you have to worry about "what happens if you get caught," don't do it.

Category Leaders Know What They Are Franchising And How To Franchise

"Success doesn't come to you . . . you go to it."

Marva Collins

51.   Peace of Mind

You may think you are in the business of providing pizza, leak detection, or some other type of product or service. You're not. In reality you are in the business of providing customers with peace of mind.

For example, you're in a hurry, but need to feed the kids dinner and get them to soccer practice. You therefore order a Little Caesars pizza, and with that pizza, you get the peace of mind of knowing that your order is going to be correct, the pizza is going to be hot, and you won't be late in getting your kids to practice.

Takeaway: Category leaders are in the business of providing customers with peace of mind.

52.   A Few Characteristics

A few characteristics of great category leaders:

(a) They do not simply offer a product or service. They offer something more – an experience, a valuable name, a secret recipe, a patented product or a truly unique operating system.

(b) They know they cannot be all things to all people. They therefore target and seek to dominate a niche such as service, quality, speed, price, convenience, or value.

(c) They are passionate about the value they provide their customers.

(d) They continue to reinvent themselves, yet stay true to their core strengths.

Takeaway: Category leaders offer more by dominating a niche and being passionate about it.

53. Franchise Expansion Models

Category leaders chose the best and most appropriate expansion model for them. There are a variety of such models, including:

(a) unit franchising
(b) area development
(c) area representation
(d) sub/master franchising

As for which model is best, each presents its own set of advantages and disadvantages.

For example, some models may result in more rapid expansion than others. Some will allow the franchisor to retain much control over unit level franchisees and others will not. Some models will result in the franchisor receiving higher upfront fees but will usually require the franchisor to share ongoing unit level franchise fees and royalty revenue. Each model also presents various issues of regulatory compliance.

Takeaway: Category leaders chose the best and most appropriate expansion model for them. Please see the Appendix for a quick "what you need to know" on each of these models.

54. Regrets, I've Had A Few

I've never heard a franchisor regret licensing a franchisee with too "small" of an exclusive "territory."

Takeaway: When in doubt, category leaders will license a smaller territory with options for expansion based on achievement of quantifiable targets.

55. Large or Small

As a franchisor, do you want a larger number of small franchisees or a smaller number of large franchisees?

Takeaway: With a larger number of small franchisees, you may have a lot of problems, but those problems are usually small. With a smaller number of large franchisees, you may have fewer problems, but those problems are usually large.

56. Predictable In Any Language

Typical international franchisor expansion pattern:

- Franchisor takes a candidate from just about any country

- Franchisor charges a very large upfront fee

- Franchisor provides international franchisee (who is to be a master franchisor/developer) with same unit-level training that franchisor provides to U.S. unit level franchisees

- After training, franchisor provides minimal ongoing support

Predictable results follow.

Takeaway: When deciding to "go" international, category leaders take the time to create a plan. They outline their target countries. They understand the culture and how business is done in those countries. They develop specific criteria to evaluate international candidates. Then, they develop the proper initial training and ongoing support systems. To succeed internationally, discipline, planning and execution are critical.

57.   The Criteria

In reviewing possible countries for international expansion, consider:

(a) Whether, in that country, there is a market for the franchisor's products or services.

(b) If there is a market, the size of that market.

(c) The level of economic freedom that consumers in that foreign market enjoy.

(d) Whether operating the franchised business in that foreign market presents any cultural, legal or other concerns and if so the nature and extent of those concerns (e.g., currency risks, potential governmental corruption and/or governmental involvement in proposed franchised business.)

Takeaway: Category leaders don't expand internationally in an indiscriminate way.

58. Do What You Do Best, Outsource The Rest

Franchisees should do what they do best and have everything else outsourced. Becoming experts in accounting, book-keeping, perhaps marketing and other non-core functions may take your franchisees away from direct revenue generating activities. Franchisors should consider the same rules of outsourcing.

Takeaway: Do what you do best and outsource the rest.

Category Leaders
Have A More Effective
Relationship With Their Franchisees

"To manage a system effectively, you might focus on the interactions of the parts rather than their behavior taken separately."

Russell L. Ackoff

59.   Best Definition of Franchising

Some define franchising as a means of distributing a product or service. Others define franchising in the context of a franchisor licensing its name and system to a franchisee in return for fees.

But, the best definition of a franchising: *a relationship between the franchisor and franchisee to service a customer.*

Takeaway: For a franchisor and franchisee to have an effective relationship, they must understand that their common purpose is to ultimately serve another.

60. Align Objectives

Franchisees usually pay royalties on their gross sales, not their net income. As such, franchisees believe or perceive that franchisors only care about their sales and not their profits.

Make sure your franchisees know what you already know:

"The franchisor's bottom line depends on the franchisee's bottom line."

Takeaway: The "bottom-line" *is* the "bottom-line." Category leaders align their objectives accordingly.

61. Best Franchisee Interview Question

Having attended hundreds of new franchisee candidate interviews, I seem to find more out about a candidate from his response to one question: "How do you feel about attending our 6-week training program?"

Takeaway: Think hard about approving candidates who tell you how much they already "know" about your business. Think even harder about making exceptions to your training requirements.

62.   It's Easy, But It's Hard

At American Leak Detection, we find water and other leaks non-invasively, which means that we do not have to bash holes in walls or dig up floors. When meeting with potential franchise candidates, employees and technicians, this is easy to explain – "leak detection without destruction."

While easy to explain, the work is hard and requires study, intelligence, and dedication.

Takeaway: Being upfront and not confusing what you do with how you do it ensures better selection of franchise candidates.

63. "Used to Be"

When you interview potential franchisee candidates, be wary of those that "used to be" franchisees of competitive franchise systems. Prior patterns and problems that may have occurred with former franchisors have ways of repeating.

Takeaway: Be wary of a "used to be."

64. Going, Going, Gone

Most franchisees go out of business not because they are technically deficient. Rather, they go *out* of business because they don't know how to *run* a business.

Takeaway: Make sure your franchisees know how to run a business, both technically, operationally and financially.

65.   No Thank You

When not accepting a franchise candidate, many times it's best not to explain. Just politely reject.

Takeaway: Sometimes no explanation is better.

66.   Forget Trust, Sort Of

Many believe that the foundation of the franchise relationship is trust. Certainly, it is important for franchisees to personally trust and like the franchisor, its founder, CEO, executives and personnel.

What is more important, however, is that franchisees trust the competency and ability of the franchisor to get the job done, set the vision, and create and execute on the plan.

Takeaway: Category leaders should focus less time on the former type of personal trust and more time on the latter type of trust pertaining to accomplishment of specific system-wide objectives.

67.   Tactics v. Strategy

"Sales are down," says the franchisee. "I better do more direct mail, or stay open late on Thursdays, or start a new promotion, or [insert tactic here]."

These tactics may be great ideas and may result in higher sales.

But before proceeding with "tactics," re-examine your overall operational, marketing and business strategy.

Takeaway: Category leaders don't let tactics define their strategy. First, they define their strategy. Then, they identify their tactics.

68.   The Franchisee Is Always Right, Right?

The franchisee is not always right but the franchisee is always human. While treating all of your franchisees alike may be difficult at times, it should not be difficult to always treat your franchisees with respect.

Takeaway: You never lose by treating your franchisees respectfully.

69.   Empty Seats

An airplane that flies with empty seats can never make up that lost revenue. The same is true with your franchisee's business. Having a busy Friday doesn't necessarily make up for a slow Wednesday.

Takeaway: Category leaders know that labor management and revenue generation are daily disciplines.

70.   The Quick Fix

In searching for the quick fix, many franchise systems believe that new and improved marketing is the answer to their sales issues. Often, however, it's not. Better operations and improved training is the answer to their sales issues.

Takeaway: Beware of the quick fix.

71. What You Market

You are rolling out a new marketing promotion. For a service business, let's say you're marketing your ability to service customers 24/7. For a product business, let's say you're marketing your newest creation, a graham-cracker flan with blueberries, raspberries, kiwi, with just a bit of crème-cheese filling.

Just a couple of problems. For your service business, you haven't been able to consistently provide 24/7 availability.

As for the flan, it tastes great. But, it takes too long to make and disrupts your restaurant's operational flow. As such, the staff hates making it and they don't even bother to mention it to customers.

Takeaway: Nothing good happens when your newest marketing promotion only serves to highlight your operational inefficiencies. Category leaders make sure that Marketing and Operations talk often.

72. Never Bet

Sales are slow. So – let's engage in a very large, clever and expensive marketing campaign – television/radio and billboard.

Well, that didn't work. So – let's engage in another expensive, large and clever marketing campaign.

Well, that didn't work. So . . . .

Takeaway: Category leaders never bet their entire sales strategy on the "next" big marketing campaign.

73.   Distressed Sales

In a distressed franchisee situation, where the existing franchisee is selling to another to avoid closing or filing bankruptcy, a franchisor may be more likely to compromise on its criteria in approving the new franchisee.

Takeaway: If you must compromise on your approval process, then over-disclose, over-train, over-help and over-document.

74. Inconsistencies, So What

Frequently, you will be told that you must make a decision a certain way to maintain "consistency." Don't believe it. Almost every situation can be distinguished. When legitimate differences exist, make the decision that is in the best interest of the franchise system.

Conversely, identify and communicate those "rules" to which there are no exceptions. Enforcing a "no-exceptions" policy and accepting the consequences can be very liberating.

Takeaway: Category leaders learn to live with inconsistencies.

75.　Fewer Choices

To get buy-in from your system, franchisees need to be able to exercise control and make choices. The key to getting anyone, however, to make a choice is to give them fewer options, not more.

Takeaway: The greater the options, the greater the paralysis.

76.   The Manual

Condense your 6-volume systems manual to 50-75 pages and distribute it for use. Keep your old manual for reference.

Takeaway: Make your manuals useable.

77.　Avoid the Bad Space

Many franchisees start with one unit, restaurant or truck. They then grow to two, three and beyond. At some point, there is not enough revenue to cover the increased overhead – yet the franchisee is personally unable to manage and supervise the additional units.

Therefore, before approving your franchisee for a third unit (which may fall into the "bad space"), discuss the financial and operational challenges with him. Then, have him prepare a financial and operational plan for movement into units 4 and 5.

Takeaway: Category leaders know their franchisee's "bad space" and help him get out of it as soon as possible.

78.   The Martha Mitchell Syndrome

The White House is engaging in illegal activities said Martha Mitchell, wife of President Nixon's Attorney General, John Mitchell. At the time, her claims were attributed to mental illness. After Watergate, her claims were verified. The mistaken process of diagnosing a patient's perception of real events as delusional is now named after Mrs. Mitchell.

You may have employees or franchisees who seem to do nothing but complain. When they raise a complaint, you may mistakenly attribute the complaint to their personality, saying, "That's just Bob" or "You know how Keith is."

That would be a mistake. Even those who complain about everything may at times raise a "complaint" that is spot-on and needs addressing.

Takeaway: Don't characterize anyone, especially your employees or franchisees.

79.   (+1) + (-1) Does Not Equal 0

You've just helped out your franchisee; perhaps it was marketing, operational or some other type of support.

The next time you see the franchisee, you expect him to thank you. He doesn't.

Instead, for what seems like the 18th time, he raises the same problem, slight or perceived slight he had with you or someone in your organization, a problem that (a) happened 5, 10 or 15 years ago; and (b) one that you've already discussed, acknowledged or tried to make right on numerous occasions.

The reason your franchisee can't "let go" of the problem is because (+1) + (-1) does not equal 0.

Stated another way: every time a franchisee deals with the franchisor, the franchisee is left with a positive or negative impression of the franchisor. The critical point for the franchisor and its staff to understand is that one positive impression does not make up for one negative impression. In these cases, negative impressions carry more weight – such that it may take 8, 10 or 12 positive impressions to make the 1 negative impression "go away."

This is where "banked" trust can be useful. If you worked really hard to ensure a positive customer experience, a slip-up later on will more easily be forgiven. Additionally, franchisees need to understand that the same "math" applies to them, both in their dealings with the franchisor and with their customers.

Takeaway: Negative impressions carry more weight.

80. Franchise Associations -- Why

If your franchisees "suddenly" form their own franchise association, remember that:

(a) The formation of an independent franchisee association usually occurs because those franchisees believe that the franchisor is either not listening to them or does not care about their concerns.

(b) The leaders of the association will usually commit to providing their "members" with more rapid and positive action on those concerns than the franchisor.

Takeaway: If your franchisees haven't yet formed their own "independent" association, don't wait for them to do so. Category leaders help with the formation of an advisory council where franchisees select their own representatives. Then, category leaders listen and address their concerns.

81. Franchise Associations – What *To* Do and What *Not* to Do

If an independent franchise association has been formed, a franchisor *should*

- communicate

- advocate its position

- take action to redress grievances

- let the system know that the franchisor's actions will always be based what is best for the entire system, and not what is best for any individual franchisee or any single franchisee group or association

A franchisor should *not*:

- threaten franchisees with any form of punishment if they join the association

- promise or grant benefits to those franchisees who do not join the association

- play favorites, alienate franchisees, or make a "martyr" of the association founders

Takeaway: If your franchisees have formed an independent association, then there are likely problems that need addressing in your system. Don't make matters worse, however, by making threats or playing favorites.

82.   Beware of the "Toxic" Franchisee

Occasionally there exists the very rare franchisee that is "toxic."

A franchisee is NOT toxic simply because a franchisee is (a) out of compliance; (b) in default; (c) high maintenance; (d) complains about everything (legitimate or not); (e) a free-rider; or (f) even brings suit against the franchisor.

So, what is a toxic franchisee? Well, what is a toxin? A toxin is a poison. When it comes into contact with an organism, that organism needs timely treatment or it will become ill and perhaps die.

Similarly, a toxic franchisee is a type of poison – it seeks, through words and conduct to come into contact with a host franchise system and cause that system illness or death.

While rare, toxic franchisees have several characteristics in common, especially arrogance. They have a need to be right, a need to act superior, and a need to be recognized as important. They are usually threatened when new ideas come from others and cannot let go of their own issues.

While patterns vary, toxic franchisees are often in compliance with the franchise agreement. But the toxic franchisee is not happy being a compliant franchisee. Essentially, the toxic franchisee wants and needs to be the franchisor, wants to make the so-called "rules" and run the so-called "show." And if the toxic franchisee cannot make the rules and run the show, it would rather bring the franchise system down.

So, how do you deal with the toxic franchisee? Some would say you should meet with the toxic franchisee, discuss grievances and attempt to resolve. But if you were really dealing with a substance that was toxic, would you ever meet with the toxin and risk contact?

Others would say you should go after the toxic franchisee. But, let's say you were bitten and there is a toxin in your system. If you called a doctor, would that doctor ever advise you that the first thing you should do is go after what bit you?

The first advice from a doctor would be to detox.

In other words, for the franchisor that has been in contact with a toxic franchisee, don't lose focus of your primary objective. That objective is the continued financial and operational health of your franchise system.

A doctor may thereafter advise you to stay away from the toxic substance. As a franchisor, you too may wish to minimize your contact or even marginalize the toxic franchisee. In doing so, you are depriving the toxic franchisee of what it seeks most of all – attention.

Ultimately, the franchisor who wants to rid itself of the toxic franchisee may not be satisfied with this advice. After all, the toxin is still in the system. Yet, what do you do, especially if the toxic franchisee is in compliance with the franchise agreement?

The answer is always the same:

DO NOTHING.

That's right; do nothing. The toxic franchisee can't help himself. At some point in the future, whether it's 6 months or 6 years, the toxic franchisee's arrogance gets the better of him. He overreaches. He believes the rules no longer apply to him. And he does something, usually stupid, which permits you to terminate the franchise agreement. The climax to this drama is actually rather anti-climatic.

Takeaway: Unfortunately the antidote for a toxic franchisee is patience. If you don't have patience, you can always offer to buy him or her out. The lesson is the same though; bad franchisee choices are costly.

83.   Hawthorne and Franchising

If you change environmental conditions you'll change behavior – at least that was the initial conclusion of Henry Landsberger. His experiments showed that better lighting and other changes in the workplace resulted in improved productivity. Yet, the improvements were short-lived.

Later, in what is now known as the "Hawthorne Effect," Landsberger concluded that it was not the lighting that caused the workers to improve their performance. Rather, performance improved simply because the workers knew that they were being observed.

Landsberger's study has been subsequently criticized. Yet, I think we've all witnessed improvement in a franchisee if, for no other reason, than the franchisee knew he was being watched and observed.

Takeaway: Category leaders observe their franchisees and give them attention. Like the Hawthorne Effect, it can't hurt.

84.   Form Over Substance, Yes

Many times form is more important than substance. Good ideas are more likely to be executed on if you follow established or agreed-upon communication, training and roll-out procedures with your system.

Takeaway: Sometimes form is more important than substance.

85. Escalation

Many times, a franchisor needs to take corrective action with a franchisee, be it a default, a termination or other issue. The franchisor, however, may be concerned that the standard 30-day notice period will simply escalate the matter, forcing both sides into a quick show-down resulting in claims and counterclaims. Doing nothing, however, may result in the franchisor waiving its rights to enforce system standards and encourage other franchisees to engage in similar wrongful conduct.

Takeaway: There are times when you need to *de-escalate.* In those cases, consider just picking up the phone and calling your franchisee to discuss the problem. When you do need to document a problem, then don't always be tied to standard 30-day notice periods. Instead, consider providing a longer period of notice, such as 180 days. By providing increased notice, you have documented the issue, avoided a quick show down, and have ideally allowed sufficient time for a real resolution.

86.   You May Have Lost More Than You Thought

Enforcing post-termination obligations (e.g., confidentiality and non-competition provisions) in the U.S. is sometimes difficult. Enforcing post-termination obligations outside of the U.S. is sometimes impossible.

When terminating a franchisee, you'll lose any existing ongoing revenue stream. Your real loss, however, may be the loss of your confidential information, trade secrets, trademarks and systems.

Takeaway: Select your franchisees carefully.

87.   Franchise Convention Success Formula

Drinks and golf are nice.

But if you want your Franchise Conference to be successful then you must provide:

(a) Content

(b) Content

(c) Content

Takeaway: Category leaders know that content always wins.

88. You Have Three Choices

When the overall economic outlook becomes uncertain, you have three choices.

First, you can be arrogant by relying on your company's history or brand and steadfastly denying that your company or industry faces any real danger.

Second, you can panic. You could do this by cancelling your convention and every meeting and program you have scheduled with your franchisees. Alternatively, you could over-schedule meetings and visits and seek to implement too many new product and service offerings.

Lastly (and what you should do) is simply take a systematic and balanced approach to any downturn. Use that time as an opportunity to renew and revitalize your brand.

Takeaway: In a downturn, category leaders take a balanced and systematic approach.

89. In a Downturn, Business Becomes Real Simple

In a downturn, business becomes real simple as there are only two items you need to look at – revenue and expenses. On the revenue side, find ways to retain your current customers, gain share from your competitors and tap into adjacent or related markets. On the expense side, cut and reduce all unnecessary items.

Takeaway: Business becomes real simple during a downturn.

90.   Buying Cooperatives

Before your franchisees form a independent buying cooperative, make sure you have written specifications for your products, manufacturers and distributors.

Takeaway: Having written specifications in advance can help avoid claims that a franchisor is acting arbitrary.

91.   Second Most Important Agreement

As a franchisor, your second most important agreement is your "Release." When you "give" something to your franchisee that you are not required to, such as permitting them to correct repeated compliance issues, approving a new store, an ownership change or granting renewal, or when you provide your franchisee with financing, have your franchisee sign a Release. The franchisee you least expect to bring suit sometimes does.

Takeaway: Find ways to use Releases often.

92. The Harmless Continuing Jurisdiction Clause

If you do not have significant experience before a particular judge or court, then re-think including a boilerplate "continuing jurisdiction" clause before that same judge or court when entering into a settlement agreement. The judge or court you don't really know may end up surprising you for a long, long time.

Takeaway: Be aware of routine or boiler-plate legal provisions.

93. Include Both

In a settlement agreement, a confidentiality clause is different than a clause stating that no party shall issue any press releases. There are times when you need to specifically include both.

Takeaway: Some clients like press and others do not. Make sure you know your client's preferences and act accordingly.

94.   I Feel Your Pain

How many hurdles do your franchisees have to go through to implement a new franchisor product or service offering? If you want your franchisees to implement a new offering, make it painless for them to do so.

Similarly, how many hurdles do your customers have to go through for the privilege of buying your products or services? If you want your franchisees to have more customers, then create systems to make it painless for customers to buy from them.

Takeaway: Category leaders make it painless for franchisees and customers to do business with them.

95. This Is Pizza

For many years, I was Vice President and General Counsel at Little Caesars Pizza. When I joined American Leak Detection, I offered new ideas and suggestions. In response, some reminded me that "this isn't pizza." I've now learned everything is pizza, as our market and business challenges are the same.

Takeaway: Our business challenges are all similar.

Appendix

a. Unit Franchising – What You Need to Know

Definition: Unit franchising is the most basic of the franchising models. The franchisor grants the franchisee the right to operate one unit at a specific location or within a defined territory. Examples include Little Caesars Pizza, American Leak Detection and Chem-Dry.

Advantages: The franchisor keeps all royalties and fees and retains complete control over the franchise system. The ability of any one franchisee to significantly impact the entire system is minimized. Additionally, because there is only one franchise agreement and disclosure document, registration and disclosure issues are much more basic and manageable than in other franchise models.

Disadvantages: The pace of growth in unit-level franchising can be slower than in other models. The franchisor is also usually working with "owner-operator" franchisees who may be less experienced in business and less financially sound than franchisees of other growth models. Lastly, the greater number of franchisees usually means higher franchisor management, supervision, training and support costs.

Takeaway: Unit franchising – slow but steady.

b. Area Development – What You Need To Know

Definition: In an area development relationship, the franchisee (called an "area developer") is granted the right to operate multiple units within a defined territory over a certain time period.

Usually, the area developer pays the franchisor a "development fee," a portion of which may be credited against future franchise fees for new units the area developer must open. Occasionally, this model has been referred to as "area franchising," "multi-unit franchising," and "multi-unit development." Examples include Panera Bread, Qdoba, Applebee's and Country Hearth Inn.

Advantages: An area development growth model may permit more rapid expansion and still provide the franchisor with system control. The franchisor usually receives a higher up-front franchise fee although a portion of those fees are credited against future units. Because there are fewer franchisees in the system (each franchisee with an "area" to develop), the franchisor's administration, training and support costs are usually reduced. Franchise registration and disclosure obligations are manageable, as there is generally one disclosure document that will contain both the franchise agreement and development agreement.

Disadvantages: Because the franchisor is locking up an "area" with one area developer, he risks "losing" the area for a certain time period if the developer fails to meet the development schedule. Moreover, an area developer's failure in an "area" or "market" may have a greater negative effect on the system than would the failure of a single unit. Because the financial and operational qualifications to be an area developer are more strenuous, the franchisor usually attracts fewer qualified area developer applicants. Those applicants may also be able to negotiate or demand greater concessions from the franchisor than unit-level franchisee applicants. Lastly, to the extent that the area developer's "development area" encompasses more than one state, several state registration and disclosure laws may be applicable to the relationship.

Takeaway: With area development, quicker growth is possible with associated moderate risk.

c. Area Representation – What You Need To Know

Definition: In an area representation model, the franchisor still signs a single-unit franchise agreement with a franchisee. The franchisor, however, *delegates* certain of its obligations to an "area representative." These obligations may include the area representative soliciting prospective franchisees on behalf of the franchisor or performing operational services for franchisees that would otherwise typically be performed by the franchisor, such as training, ongoing consultation and enforcement of system standards. At times, area representatives have been referred to as "area directors," "regional directors," "masters," and "development agents." Examples include Taco Del Mar, Subway and Blimpies.

Advantages: Rapid system development is possible. The franchisor also retains direct contractual control with unit level franchisees. Because there is only a single disclosure document, registration issues are not burdensome. Additionally, system changes may be easier to implement.

Disadvantages: The biggest disadvantage (or difficultly) is that the franchisor must be able to train, and the area representative must be able to learn, how to perform services traditionally performed by the franchisor, including soliciting potential franchisees, training new franchisees, attending grand openings, providing continued support to franchisees through field visits and ensuring that system standards are maintained. As compensation to the area representative, the franchisor usually shares a portion of its franchise fees and royalties, thereby reducing long-term revenue that would otherwise be earned by the franchisor. If the area representative fails to comply with disclosure obligations, there is potential liability for the franchisor. Additionally, since the unit-level franchisee is primarily dealing with the area representative, the franchisor may not become aware of serious system problems until later stages, negatively affecting ability of the franchisor to provide corrections. Lastly, the termination of an area representative may result in the franchisor being obligated to service franchisees in a territory without having adequate infrastructure.

Takeaway: With area representation, quicker development is possible through delegation with loss of some control and fee sharing.

d. Sub-Franchising/Master-Franchising – What You Need To Know

Definitions: In a sub-franchising model, the franchisor grants a sub-franchisor the right to license units to sub-franchisees. Typically, two agreements exist – one between the franchisor and sub-franchisor (or sub) and a separate agreement between the sub-franchisor and sub-franchisee (or unit level franchisee.)

A variation of sub-franchising is master-franchising, which is more commonly used internationally. Like sub-franchising, a master will sub-franchise units and provide sub-franchisees with services that are typically provided by a franchisor. Additionally, a master will usually open a number of its own units that it will continue to operate. Examples include Cartridge World, Blenz Coffee, GMAC Real Estate.

Advantages: A tremendous rate of expansion and development is possible. The franchisor usually receives higher upfront fees from the sub or master. The franchisor is also not responsible for day-to-day training, supervision or other support functions of the sub-franchisees, as the franchisor is permitted to focus on more efficient activities such as securing national accounts, national advertising, research and development, and matters involving purchasing and distribution. Because of the fewer overall number of sub-franchisees, the franchisor's administrative and support costs are also usually lower.

Disadvantages: A substantial investment is required on part of sub-franchisor, thereby reducing the number of qualified applicants. Additionally, many of the sub-franchisor's costs are front-loaded, with a return on investment usually deferred. The franchisor shares sub-franchisee royalties and initial fees with the sub. Additionally, because there are higher costs and fees involved, there may be cases where these fees are passed on to unit-level franchisees, making investment less attractive, competitive or viable.

Other disadvantages include that the franchisor may not have a proven ability to teach, and the sub-franchisor may not have proven ability to learn, how to perform franchisor-like services. There may also be times where system-wide costs are inefficiently high due to each sub-franchisor being required to provide all support functions.

The ability to effectively control sub-franchisee's operations can also be lost by the franchisor, meaning that the franchisor may also lose the ability to control and guide the entire system. If the agreement between the franchisor and the sub-franchisor is terminated, there may be difficulties in dealing with the sub-franchisees. While the unit level agreements may be automatically assigned to franchisor, until such time, the franchisor has had no direct contractual relationship with the sub-franchisees and there may not be adequate infrastructure in place for providing continuing support.

Registration and disclosure complexities also exist as a result of double disclosure (franchisor and sub-franchisor required to have separate disclosure documents; both required to have audited financials - each with resulting legal and other costs.) Finally, the franchisor may have increased legal risks. For example, the franchisor may be jointly and severally liable for a master's or sub's violation of registration/disclosure laws. There is also an increased risk of the franchisor being held "vicariously liable" for acts of the master or sub-franchisor.

Takeaway: With sub-franchising, very rapid growth is possible as are higher fees along with higher risks and potential downside.

Acknowledgments

I thank those that have offered their advice and guidance over the years including Kay Ainsley, Irwin Alterman, Nancy Bartlett, Marty Caruso, Bill Crystler, Stuart deGeus, Dr. R. Engel, Dennis Evoe, John Forrest, Carolyn Gough, David Gray, Bob Gappa, Barry Heller, Marian Ilitch, Chris Ilitch, Linda Jaworski, Jim Johnson, William Killion, Steve King, John Kotlar, Ed Kushell, David Kushner, Robert Mazziotti, Jerry Pasternak, Michael Scruggs, Michael Seid, Charlie Sciandra, David Scrivano, Mike Scruggs, Mike Shaub, Darryl Snygg, John Tifford, Michael Therrian, Brett Yates, colleagues, friends and franchisees of American Leak Detection, Inc. and Little Caesar Enterprises, Inc.

In addition to their advice and guidance over the years, I thank the following for some of the thoughts, ideas and solutions contained in this book: Barry Barnes (thoughts relating to ch24), Patrick DeSouza (thoughts relating to ch95), Bill Edwards (thoughts relating to ch56); Tom Feltenstein (thoughts relating to ch37), Darryl Johnson (thoughts relating to ch77), Michael Ilitch (thoughts relating to ch32), Stan Moore (thoughts relating to ch80-81), Arthur Pressman (thoughts relating to ch6), Dr. Tom Steiner (thoughts relating to ch51), Michael Treacy (thoughts relating to ch88) and Edith Wiseman (thoughts relating to ch53, Appendix, a-d.)

Finally, special appreciation to Kristen Johnson for all of her help.

Of course, the contents and views expressed herein are mine and do not necessarily represent the views or opinions of others.

Author Biography

Stan Berenbaum is president and CEO of American Leak Detection, Inc., an international franchisor that leads the category in non-invasive leak detection and related services. As an attorney, author, speaker and business and franchise executive, Mr. Berenbaum has helped companies thrive as category leaders for over 15 years.

Prior to joining American Leak Detection, Mr. Berenbaum was Vice President and General Counsel of Little Caesar Enterprises, Inc., and a partner in the Antitrust and Trade Regulation Department of the Honigman Miller law firm in Detroit, Michigan.

Mr. Berenbaum received his undergraduate (*summa cum laude*) and law degree (*cum laude*) from Wayne State University. He received his Certificate in Executive Leadership from Cornell University. In addition to being a Certified Franchise Executive, Mr. Berenbaum is a member of the National Advisory Board of the Franchise Center at the University of Texas at El Paso as well as a member of The National Speakers Association and the International Coach Federation.

Mr. Berenbaum is licensed to practice law before a variety of courts, including the Sixth Circuit Court of Appeals, the Ninth Circuit Court of Appeals, as well as the U.S. Supreme Court. Mr. Berenbaum has written, spoken and lectured on a number of franchising, business and antitrust topics.

Mr. Berenbaum, his wife and family live in Palm Desert, California.

Contact Us

We're interested in your thoughts, experiences, suggestions and feedback. Please contact us at:

spb@StanBerenbaum.com

www.StanBerenbaum.com

Printed in the United States
146995LV00002B/5/P

9 781440 132285